MOUNT RUSHMORE

AMERICAN SYMBOLS

Lynda Sorensen

The Rourke Book Company, Inc.
Vero Beach, Florida 32964

PHOTO CREDITS
Courtesy of South Dakota Tourism: cover, pages 4, 8, 10, 15, 18;
courtesy of National Park Service: title page, pages 12 (Lincoln
Borglum), 13, 17, 21 (Paul Horsted); © Lynn Stone; page 7

Library of Congress Cataloging-in-Publication Data

Sorensen, Lynda, 1953-–
     Mount Rushmore / by Lynda Sorensen
         p. cm. — (American symbols)
     Includes index.
     ISBN 1-55916-047-0
     1. Mount Rushmore National Memorial (S.D.)—Juvenile literature.
[1. Mount Rushmore National Memorial (S.D.) 2. National
monuments.] I. Title. II. Series.
F657.R8S67   1994
978.3'93—dc20   94–7053
                                              CIP
                                              AC

Printed in the USA

TABLE OF CONTENTS

MOUNT RUSHMORE

They died long ago, but four of America's greatest presidents still "live" on Mount Rushmore.

The likenesses of the presidents are carved into the mountain rock. Much larger than life, the great stone faces stare at the Black Hills of South Dakota.

Like the presidents themselves, the heads of stone have become **symbols** of American ideals.

Gone but not forgotten, four United States presidents still stand tall in the Black Hills of South Dakota

FACES IN THE ROCK

The stone faces on Mount Rushmore remind people of more than just four presidents. They are symbols of what those four presidents stood for.

George Washington was known for his courage and battlefield skill. His leadership led to America's freedom from England in 1783.

Abraham Lincoln is remembered for his firm belief in a united nation and freedom for everyone.

Thomas Jefferson wrote much of America's Declaration of Independence. Teddy Roosevelt was a champion of natural resources.

From left to right: Washington, Jefferson, T.R. Roosevelt, Lincoln

ROBINSON'S IDEA

The idea of faces in granite rock of the Black Hills was Doane Robinson's. Robinson was South Dakota's state **historian**. He wanted the faces of Western heroes, such as Kit Carson, in the Needles. The Needles is a jumble of tall, pointed rocks in Custer State Park.

Robinson invited a **sculptor**, Gutzon Borglum, to the Black Hills in 1924. Sculptors carve or model subjects in such things as bronze, copper, clay and rock.

Faces in granite—the idea of Doane Robinson—loom behind a visitor to Mount Rushmore

BORGLUM'S BETTER IDEA

Borglum had a better idea. Why not, he said, make a memorial of interest to all Americans?

Borglum wanted to carve the images of presidents instead of frontier heroes. The idea took off.

Borglum chose Mount Rushmore as a work **site**, or location, in place of the Needles. Rushmore faced the sun most of the day. At 5,725 feet above sea level, it stood well above the land nearby. And the sculptor knew he could shape the smooth granite face of Mount Rushmore.

Sunshine plays on the snowy faces
of the presidents

Lincoln Borglum stands atop studio model of the presidents

The presidents dwarf a helicopter

SHAPING A MOUNTAIN'S FACE

Bringing the images of four presidents to Mount Rushmore was a giant task. The faces were too huge to be actually carved. The rocks would have to be shaped by removing sections of the rock with dynamite.

Borglum's workers began the project on August 10, 1927. President Calvin Coolidge made Mount Rushmore a national memorial on the same day.

On safety ropes, a National Park Service worker visits Lincoln for the annual cleaning of the carvings

THE NEW FACES ON THE MOUNTAIN

Workmen drilled holes in the rock to plant dynamite. Before the job was completed, 450,000 tons of Mount Rushmore had been blasted away.

As if by magic, the faces of four presidents began to appear in the granite. Finally, in 1941 the job was finished. Gutzon Borglum died early in 1941, leaving his son Lincoln to finish the project.

Gutzon Borglum's work on Mount Rushmore was nearly finished when this photo was taken in 1941

THE FACES OF GIANTS

If the four presidents are giants in American history, they are no less giants on the mountain.

Each head averages 60 feet from chin to top, the height of a five-story apartment. The mouths average 18 feet across. Each nose is about 20 feet long.

Borglum loved super-sized carvings. But he explained that they should be saved only for people and events that were of giant importance.

A worker is little more than a mosquito on the carving of President Theodore R. Roosevelt

MOUNTAIN MEN

Just who are those men on the mountain?

George Washington became the first president after leading the American army to victory against the British (1775-1783).

Thomas Jefferson was the nation's third president, an inventor and the founder of the University of Virginia. Lincoln, as president, held the nation together during America's Civil War (1861-1865).

President Theodore Roosevelt (1901-1909) created the first national forests and wildlife refuges.

Spotlights shine on the presidents each night during Mount Rushmore's summer season

VISITING MOUNT RUSHMORE

A short trail from the Visitor Center at Mount Rushmore National Memorial offers a grand view of the mountain. Other short trails through the 1,278 acres of pine woods also lead to mountain views.

Mount Rushmore is 25 miles southwest of Rapid City and two miles from Keystone, South Dakota. The memorial has no lodges or campgrounds. Visitors make day trips.

Glossary

historian (hih STOR ee an) — someone who studies the written history, or record, of people of the past

sculptor (SKULP tor) — an artist who carves works of art from rock, clay or some other material

site (SITE) — a location, place

symbol (SIM bull) — something which stands for something else, as a flag stands for a country

INDEX

OAKLAND MEDIA CENTER